Anna Ziegler

ACTUALLY

9781786823083

OBERON BOOKS
LONDON

WWW.OBERONBOOKS.COM

First published in 2017 by Oberon Books Ltd
521 Caledonian Road, London N7 9RH
Tel: +44 (0) 20 7607 3637 / Fax: +44 (0) 20 7607 3629
e-mail: info@oberonbooks.com
www.oberonbooks.com

Reprinted with revisions in 2018

Anna Ziegler is hereby identified as author of this play
in accordance with section 77 of the Copyright, Designs and
Patents Act 1988. The author has asserted their moral rights.

A catalogue record for this book is available from the British
Library.

PB ISBN: 9781786823083
E ISBN: 9781786823090

Cover image: RabbitWayne

eBook conversion by CPI Group (UK) Ltd, Croydon, CR0 4YY.

Visit www.oberonbooks.com to read more about all our books
and to buy them. You will also find features, author interviews and
news of any author events, and you can sign up for e-newsletters
so that you're always first to hear about our new releases.

ACTUALLY

Author's Note

As I write this note, on September 27th, 2017, the current administration in the United States has just issued interim guidance that undoes or complicates some of the previous administration's mandates around the implementation of Title IX as it relates to cases of sexual misconduct on college campuses. One of these new measures has to do with the standard of proof used to determine the outcome of these cases; while the Obama administration stipulated that this standard should be "preponderance of the evidence" (otherwise known as "fifty percent plus a feather") the current administration has suggested that schools have more leeway to decide what standard they deem appropriate. Now universities can adopt a "clear and convincing" standard, if they so choose, but preponderance of the evidence is still permissible (and in fact will likely continue to be used much of the time since it was also suggested that the same standard be applied to all campus misconduct cases – and many, if not most, colleges use preponderance of the evidence when it comes to those other kinds of cases). When I wrote this play, preponderance of the evidence was the norm. Schools risked serious repercussions if they didn't uphold the various measures set out in the "Dear Colleague" letter penned in 2011 by the Education Department under President Obama.

The backdrop against which the play was written and the backdrop against which you are reading it (whenever you are reading it) is both hugely important and also, from my point of view, beside the point. The play, to me, not only holds up a mirror to a certain moment in time (2015 or 2016, probably) but also hopefully speaks to a larger and more timeless question about who we are as men and as women and what forces drive our actions. It looks at how difficult it can be to determine what happened in a bed between two real people capable of all that humans are capable of – obfuscating, deceiving themselves, not understanding, not wanting to be impolite or to embarrass themselves, of letting need or insecurity take precedence over empathy. It asks that you consider whether "good" people can make bad mistakes – or worse. And if *Actually* is making any kind of statement, it is that one, about the quality and complications of our souls. What standard of proof is used to determine the outcome of the case is not nearly as important to me as the human question at the heart of the play.

So even if you are reading this in 2025 – or 2050, and colleges are no longer handling these kinds of cases (or if there are no more colleges!) – I'd like to think the story will still resonate. Only time will tell.

ACTUALLY was originally produced in a co-production between The Geffen Playhouse (Randall Arney, Artistic Director) and The Williamstown Theatre Festival (Mandy Greenfield, Artistic Director).

GEFFEN PLAYHOUSE

Opening night at The Geffen Playhouse was on 10 May 2017, with the following cast and creative team:

TOM	Jerry MacKinnon
AMBER	Samantha Ressler
Director	Tyne Rafaeli
Stage Manager	Liz Brohm
Set Designer	Tim Mackabee
Costume Designer	Caitlin Ward
Lighting Designer	Lap Chi Chu
Sound Designer	Vincent Olivieri

WILLIAMSTOWN THEATRE FESTIVAL

Opening night at the Williamstown Theatre Festival was on 12 August 2017, with the following cast and creative team:

TOM	Joshua Boone
AMBER	Alexandra Socha
Director	Lileana Blain-Cruz
Stage Manager	Dane Urban
Set Designer	Adam Rigg
Costume Designer	Paloma Young
Lighting Designer	Ben Stanton
Sound Designer	Jane Shaw

The Off-Broadway premiere of *ACTUALLY* was produced by The Manhattan Theatre Club (Lynne Meadow, Artistic Director; Barry Grove, Executive Producer). Opening night was on 14 November 2017, with the following cast and creative team:

TOM	Joshua Boone
AMBER	Alexandra Socha
Director	Lileana Blain-Cruz
Stage Manager	Dane Urban
Scenic Designer	Adam Rigg
Costume Designer	Paloma Young
Lighting Designer	Yi Zhao
Sound Designer	Jane Shaw

Acknowledgements

I'd like to give special thanks to Daniella Topol, Amy Levinson, Tyne Rafaeli and Lileana Blain-Cruz, all of whom put in countless hours to help me see what this play could be. Thanks also to Mandy Greenfield, Randall Arney, and Lynne Meadow for so quickly giving this play not one, but three homes! The Lark Play Development Center, The Playwrights Realm, Seth Glewen, Elizabeth Rothman, Nicki Hunter, Will Cantler, Samantha Ressler, Jerry MacKinnon, Alexandra Socha and Joshua Boone are and were invaluable. But this play would not exist if not for Will Miller, and neither, for that matter, would our children, and so to him I am eternally grateful.

Characters

AMBER
early-mid 20s, high-strung, talkative, charmingly neurotic.
She does not present as insecure. She is Jewish.

TOM
early-mid 20s, appealing and confident with some
swagger that conceals a deeper vulnerability.
He is African-American.

(Lights up on a college party. Princeton. Two students, freshmen –
AMBER and TOM – are outside on the quad. A first date. Sort of.
They're drinking. A lot.)

AMBER

So I was reading tonight in our psych book about the pratfall
effect, and it's actually really interesting: it's about how a
person's attractiveness increases or decreases after he or she
makes a mistake. So a highly-competent person, like, say,
a celebrity, would be *more* likable after committing a blunder,
while the opposite would be true if –

TOM

God, do you ever stop talking?

AMBER

What?

TOM
(With a small smile.)

Just stop talking.

AMBER

Okay.

TOM

I'm gonna kiss you now.

AMBER

Oh.
Okay.

(They do. AMBER's not sure what to do with her hand so it hovers
awkwardly over TOM's shoulder, not touching it.)

AMBER

Let's play a game. Let's play Two Truths and a Lie.

TOM
(Emphatic.)

Um. No.

AMBER

Come on.

TOM

Okay. I have two truths for you... I hate games and I hate that game.

AMBER

But you'll play it.

TOM

And why would I do that?

AMBER

If you wanna sleep with me tonight, for one thing.

TOM

(Without missing a beat.)

Who goes first?

(A sharp shift in tone. AMBER and TOM abruptly turn to face the audience.)

AMBER

So.

TOM

(To the audience.)

In some ways I've been on trial my entire life.

AMBER

It wasn't an actual trial. It was a hearing but it felt like a trial.
We sat across from each other. At these long wooden tables.
I felt like I was a character in *The Crucible.* Maybe because
our "trial" was in a classroom where I'd happened to read *The
Crucible* earlier that semester.

TOM

We sat across from each other.

AMBER

The room was very cold. I had to wear *two* layers. The cardigan I
carry with me because I am *always* cold but also my jacket. *Inside.*

TOM

I couldn't believe how cold this girl got. She'd have goose bumps like sitting outside on a 75 degree day.

(An abrupt shift back to each other, and into a continuation of the original scene.)

AMBER

Okay my first truth is: I thought I'd fall in love on my first day of college.

TOM
(That's weird.)

First day?

AMBER
(She speaks very fast.)

Well, my parents did. My dad was my mom's professor in a class called History of the American South and she liked his accent and in a sort of twisted way that he was old enough to be her father and I guess he liked being able to lord it over her and probably her looks – my mom was very attractive back then – because then they were together.

TOM

That was allowed back then?

AMBER

You don't even know if anything I just said was true.

TOM

Okay. Fair point.

AMBER

Second one: I have never excelled at any sport.

TOM

But you're on the squash team.

AMBER

Third one: I have no feelings for you whatsoever.

(TOM stares at her.)

So now you guess.

TOM

No, I know. I'm thinking.

AMBER

Lay out your thought process.

TOM

Well, I'm an arrogant bastard so I think you do like me…
And that shit about your parents is either too detailed to be
a lie or so detailed it's the obvious lie.

AMBER

Hm. Interesting.

TOM

You're on a team here so I think you've excelled at sports.
And I'm way confident you're into me –

AMBER

So you've said.

TOM

But I'll go with the lie is about your parents.

AMBER

The lie was not about my parents.

TOM

Then you're no good at sports.

AMBER

I'm no good at sports.

TOM

How the hell did you get on the squash team?

AMBER

Anyone can get on the squash team.

TOM

Is that right.

AMBER

I mean, you don't have to be great. You can be good. Or just
okay. It's a great way to help you get into college.
Just like being black.

TOM

(Incredulous and amused.)

Um. You know you can't say that. Right?

AMBER

But it's not a micro-aggression or anything.

TOM

'Cause it's like a *macro*-aggression.

AMBER

(Unapologetic, matter-of-fact.)

Come on. Everyone has things that help them get in. I'm not
saying either of us is remotely unqualified to be here.

TOM

(In disbelief.)

Wow. Okay.

AMBER

No, I'm sure you're super smart. You had to beat out a shit ton
of other black kids to get in. I just had to beat out some other
mediocre squash players.

TOM

You think my only competition was other black kids?

AMBER

Mainly, yeah. We all fill some stupid niche, which reduces us
to something much less than what we are, but that's the way
it goes. Has it been very hard for you, being black?

TOM

(Laughing.)

God, you really are, like…a piece of work.

AMBER

But has it?

(Another sharp turn out to the audience.)

AMBER

See it became, almost immediately, "the matter of Anthony dash Cohen".

(Bashfully.)

Which I couldn't help thinking looked like what our last name would be if we got married...

TOM

I get an email from the Office of the Vice Provost of Institutional Equity and Diversity. It's from some dude named Leslie. He made it clear that he was a dude by saying "because the name can be ambiguous I want to make you aware that I am a man." I'm told to come into the office at my very earliest convenience.

AMBER

What happened was I told Heather who told our RA Olivia who told whoever she told.

TOM

I honestly thought maybe this was about my being an asshole for not joining the Black Student Union.

AMBER

But I didn't know Heather would tell anyone. She just came into my room and was like "Amber. People are saying you were *topless* at Cap last night. What the fuck. Were you super wasted?" And I'm like "that's the least of it. I mean, Thomas Anthony practically raped me." And she looked at me with these wide eyes, like she was kind of seeing me for the first time... And I knew immediately that I'd said something I couldn't take back.

TOM

So I'm sitting across from Leslie, and the guy has an enormous beard. Part of me wonders if maybe there *is* a woman behind there.

AMBER

And so I tell her what happened. Or what I can remember.
But I don't tell Heather everything. I mean, why should
Heather know everything?

TOM

And he's like "I assume you know why you're here" and I'm
like "enlighten me, Leslie" not realizing I shouldn't be, like,
a dick right now. And he squints his eyes at me like he can't
believe what he's hearing.

Okay, so even though my mom was always like "don't give
anyone any reason to write you off" I'm still not great at
gauging when I really should be polite. Like in 11th grade I once
said to the school psychologist: "who's *your* shrink, shrink?"

I mean, I had this one weird thing and my high school sent me
into therapy. What's that all about?

AMBER

So I just say to Heather that things went pretty far and she's
like but that's not rape and I'm like I know that Heather.
What might have maybe constituted something approaching
sex without my one hundred percent consent was that he got
a tiny bit rough with me and at first I was into it but then I
wasn't into it anymore and I stood up and was like "actually,
um" but he pulled me back and kept going. And then she says,
all horrified "and all you said was 'actually'?" and I'm like
yeah. And she's like "but that's not no" and I'm like I know
that, Heather – I am aware that two different words in the
English language are not the same word... Also, I was just so
so drunk.

(Abrupt shift back to the scene.)

TOM

Okay, so I guess I'll say...in the spirit of truth...

AMBER

Or maybe a lie.

TOM

If I can, one day I'd like to play piano professionally. Like in a symphony. Or jazz piano. Or, like, the orchestra pit of Hamilton / or something.

AMBER

Oh god I love that show.

TOM
(Impressed.)

You saw it??

AMBER

No!

TOM

Okay… The second one is…my mom is the love of my life.

AMBER

Aw. That's sweet. That better not be a lie or you're kind of deranged.

TOM

The third one is…
I feel most out of place when people would assume I feel most comfortable.

AMBER

Like when?

TOM

You don't even know if that one's true.

AMBER
(Kind, knowing.)

I know it's true… The question is which of the other two is the lie.

TOM

Oh fuck.

AMBER

What.

8

TOM

I fucked it up.

AMBER

You forgot to lie.

TOM

I straight up told you I hate games.

AMBER

Wanna do it over?

TOM

I'm just too honest. What can I say?

AMBER
(Gentle.)
Then tell me some other things that are true.

(Beat.)

TOM
(To the audience.)
I was playing the piano in one of the music rooms during a free period. And this teacher Emily Mackey, who couldn't be more than five feet tall, and who teaches percussion, (which is like "percussion" – who even takes that?), she walks in and asks if I'd mind if she listened to me play.

I was like sure, be my guest, and I just kept playing. And yeah, maybe I stepped it up a little because I had an audience. And maybe it wasn't totally lost on me that Ms. Mackey looked about eighteen and also that she was a type I hadn't tried before – you know: boy body, flat-chested, short hair.

AMBER

But, like, who is Heather to judge because she's probably always had great sex. I bet even her first time was amazing, with, like, candles, and some guy who *worshiped* her because she probably gives head like a porn star, and I'm sure she lost her virginity in, like, 9th grade so she never had to be embarrassed, in high school, that she hadn't done it.

TOM

So when she stood up and was like leaning on the piano while I played, I might've gotten pretty fancy with my fingers, just sort of dancing them over the keys.

I don't mean to come off, like…but at the time I felt I knew a coupla things. One was that I was decent-looking. Or maybe a little better than that. And the other was that I was a damn good piano player.

And she's sort of swaying. Ms. Mackey. I'm playing Bartok's third piano concerto, which is kind of a weird one, sort of all over the place, and not always the most, like, melodious, but she's *into* it.

And then, at the end of the first movement, she sits on the bench next to me so our legs are touching. And it's this fucking electric electricity and I don't know what to do about it. So I look her in the eyes and wait a second to be sure I'm reading everything right before I kiss her.

AMBER

Whereas I was always really scared of *everything* about it. Like when I was little I remember wondering, like how you possibly get yourself into the situation where sex would actually occur. It all seemed so impossible to me, and embarrassing. And then, when you're older, you start thinking about how to *avoid* sex – because it's actually right there in front of you from 7th grade on, and that's, like terrifying. But no one *admits* that. No one admits that if you hook up with a guy but you don't go as far as he'd like, or if you go *too* far, like my friend Rachel did, then you end up on a private blog that does *not* stay private, which you definitely don't wanna be on except if you're not it means no one has noticed that you even exist.

TOM

So…the funny or maybe sad thing about Bartok's third piano concerto is that he died before he finished it. He was writing it for his wife's birthday; he was gonna surprise her and I guess he did – but not in the way he was going for.

And the funny or maybe sad thing about that afternoon when I was playing it is that Mr. Damion, the chair of the music department at Carpenter, this total walking prick – I mean, the guy literally looks like a penis – well, he walked right into the room, and there I am, on top of the tiny percussion teacher, playing her like a fucking symphony.

And…um.

The least funny thing about what happens next is that she says I came onto her. And also, that I was aggressive or something.

                    AMBER
At some point later it occurs to you that maybe sex should be a *pleasant* experience. But how to make that happen is a whole other thing. I mean, how can you control what kind of sex you're about to have? You usually don't know until you're in it. Or maybe not even 'til after it's over. Like days or weeks or even *years* in the past. Which is what I try to tell Heather, but she's very definite about things, so she's just like: if he raped you, he raped you, okay? And I'm like "okay!!"

                    TOM
I mean, credit to my mom, because she didn't believe it for a second… Said it was racism. Plain and simple. And, you know…maybe it was.
Maybe it was.

Ms. Mackey got fired, so I guess that's… But then everyone asks why she's gone so by December of my junior year, I'm the guy who fucked this sweet little teacher literally and figuratively, even though we didn't actually fuck, and I have to see this shrink because what if I'm like totally depraved, which seemed like such a joke.

                AMBER and TOM
But now

                    AMBER
I realize it's my default state. This zone of wanting something and not wanting it at the same time. And, like, what happened with Zach was a big example of that.

11

TOM

Leslie looks at me and says "this is about you and Amber
Cohen. I believe you two are acquainted." And then there's
this silence while my brain computes that. Me and Amber
Cohen. And my first thought is she did something weird, like
maybe she's in trouble for doing something really fucking
weird, but then I look at his face and I can tell it's not that.

AMBER

Zach's my friend Rachel's brother, this totally white bread
frat guy type, not the brightest bulb but *cute*, you know? And
I liked him probably in large part because he never seemed
to know who I was, even though I was over at Rachel's all the
time and always tried to look nice for him but also not like I
was *trying* to look nice because you can't seem to be trying to
look nice when you're going over to your friend's house to do
Latin homework.

TOM

And he starts talking about "Title IX" and how it's his
responsibility to oversee all investigations of conduct that
might have violated the policy. And he's speaking really
carefully and not making eye contact and it's making me
feel like I did when I was going out with this girl Alexa at
Carpenter who was actually a sort of minor celebrity – like
she had this blog that I never read but white people like Lena
Dunham were all excited about it or something? I didn't care;
she was hot and we'd go to her apartment after school and
no one was ever home and then one afternoon I was sitting
around in my *underwear* and her mother just, like, walks in
and Alexa is all, "oh this is Tom; I told you about Tom, didn't
I?" which she clearly hadn't, and the mother acts as though
she's so excited to see me there, which she clearly isn't, and
the whole thing is so uncomfortable and I sort of knew that if
I'd been a different guy she would have sent me home on the
spot but instead there I was having *dinner* with them and being
talked to like *I* was the celebrity, like they'd be so disappointed
when I'd finally have to leave.

12

AMBER

I was a senior in high school and I'd just gotten into college. Like, *that day*, I mean.

I'd come home from school and I was scrolling through this really dumb email where you have to rank like the five best books you've ever read and then send it onto the second person on the list and I was trying to decide whether to make my number one, like, *Gone Girl* or *The Iliad*, when I see I have a new email and the subject line is "Welcome to…" but you can't see the whole thing, so I open it and it's Princeton.

TOM

I'm like what policy, Leslie? I honestly don't know what he's… But then he says "sexual misconduct"… And he says it strangely loud, like he's embarrassed, which embarrasses *me*. See, I've never had any clue what to do with someone who's trying to hide how they feel…probably because *I* am always trying to hide how I feel.

AMBER

Which is… I mean, I was NOT expecting to get in. I really wasn't, even though being a mediocre squash player can help a lot because colleges need to fill their teams, and there just aren't enough really excellent squash players. But still I didn't expect anything that good to happen to me. I was always kind of not the best at anything, you know?

Like, I was never the *prettiest* girl. Not, like, ugly. I mean, I *can* actually look in the mirror and see a person who's kind of attractive, looking back at me. I don't know. My mom told me once I was "pretty enough" which one hundred percent of shrinks would probably agree explains everything.

TOM

So I'm just like…what?? And he says it even louder, even though the problem wasn't that I didn't hear him.

AMBER

The day I got into Princeton was the second night of Passover and Rachel had invited me to her family's seder. But I mean, who does the *whole* service on the SECOND night? And not only that but her dad asks everyone at the seder to discuss things, like why is it worse to be indifferent than stupid? In reference to the four sons. And why do we say next year in Jerusalem?

And before I know what I'm doing I'm looking right at Zach and saying something about Jews and longing, and I know my face is very very red and kind of splotchy. Which is what happens when I'm embarrassed, so the whole world can see exactly how I'm feeling at all times.

TOM

So, just to be clear… Amber says I violated the policy? And he says yes, she has lodged a complaint. And I'm like, "but that girl is seriously into me" and he gives me this look like I'm deluded. *(A realization.)* Which I guess I am.

AMBER

After the seder, we're all just hanging out, and Zach wants to watch hockey because the Rangers are having an okay season so they're "worth watching", but, you know, they lose. In like overtime.

And Zach is not happy. I guess he's one of those beleaguered fans who takes everything really hard, and he's like "I'm gonna have a fucking drink" which makes it sound like he hadn't *already* been drinking all night long, but now he switches to beer, even though it has barley or wheat in it or whatever and isn't something you're supposed to have during Passover. But he's just like "fuck it. The Rangers weren't supposed to lose during Passover either." Which doesn't make any sense.

TOM

I ask him: what exactly does she say I did? And what you can see of Leslie behind that beard turns this bright shade of red and he's like "she says you raped her, Thomas"…and I can't help it but I start to cry.

14

AMBER

Rachel had fallen asleep on the couch, and Zach asked if I
wanted to see this app on his phone that's like an updated
version of *Angry Birds Star Wars*, but really he just wanted me
to come sit next to him because once I was there he kind of
touched my wrist and I froze and of course he knew. I mean,
really he'd probably known

AMBER and TOM

For years

TOM

my dad was a star. A math wiz, a point guard, a model son.
But by the end of high school he was drinking, and getting into
fights, and he never made it to college, which haunted him
forever because he knew he should have. And here *I* am, at
Princeton, sitting across from Leslie, who asks what questions I
have about the rape I may or may not have committed within
the first two months of school. And then there they are too,
creeping into the corners of your mind: those men swaying in
the trees, because they're always there.

AMBER

And he stands and kind of pulls me up with him, and we go to
his room and he's kinda stumbly drunk and I am completely
sober and we fall onto the bed and he is not exactly gentle
with me but I don't really mind; the next day I get a UTI and
it hurts so bad, but I don't know that right now and eventually
he takes his fingers out of me and squeezes one of my boobs
really hard, and I moan a little because I think that's what
people do but he puts his finger to his mouth like I've made
this faux pas by making a sound, a gesture I remember at least
subconsciously because now I am always silent during sex,
always always, like you practically don't know I'm there, and
then he climbs on top of me and sticks it in. And the whole
time, which isn't a long time, I keep thinking "I got into college
today" which, in conjunction with what's happening right now,
makes me feel like a...yeah, like a different person, I guess.
And when he's done he grunts a little, like this sound is just
getting pushed out of him and it's not exactly a happy sound,

but still I feel weirdly privileged – and in all honesty, grown up – to know what Zach Lieberman sounds like when he comes.

TOM

And I just blurt out: I'm innocent until proven guilty, right? And Leslie looks kind of apologetic and then, really gently, is like: yes and no… In the coming weeks, before the hearing, there will absolutely be a comprehensive investigation… but also you should know that college campuses are not the criminal justice system. There's no judge or jury. A panel of three "neutral" appointees will interview you and Amber and any witnesses to try to get a full picture of what happened and then we will "convene" altogether and discuss. And I'm like "thanks, Leslie" and he's like "of course, Tom" so, like, I guess he thought I was being sincere.

AMBER

It snowballed. I'm suddenly the most interesting person Heather has ever met and she wants to be with me all the time. She even waits in the hall when I go talk to this guy Leslie, whom I'd just assumed was going to be a woman because of the name and also because here was someone whose job was to talk to predominantly female *rape victims*.

AMBER	TOM
But it wasn't.	But I wasn't.

TOM

And Leslie says if the panel determines that a preponderance of the evidence suggests I did it, he will be brought in to help determine my penalty. And I'm like "what??" and he says: if they find that the claim is more likely true than not true, which is still sounding kinda opaque to me, and he's like "fifty percent plus a feather – that's what it's like", and I picture this two sided scale, and each side has the same amount on it, the very same shit, but wait, what's that up there? Oh, it's a feather, and it comes drifting down from the sky…and lands on one side of the scale and suddenly that side is weighted down beyond belief. Suddenly there's no contest.

AMBER

I tell Leslie that my mom says Bob, my stepdad, *Bob* says
I have to be really careful about accusing a black man of…
you know. And the way Leslie looks at me, even though he
doesn't say anything, makes me worry that Tom isn't gonna
get a fair trial, like he's gonna be one of those black men just
tossed recklessly into the tornado of a broken system, but
then I realize that shouldn't really matter to me. I can't fix the
system, can I?

TOM

So the panel of three neutral appointees is made up of a
white dude who's like the assistant *assistant* dean of students,
this hippy-ish art professor who looks white to me but her
last name is Diaz; and a black woman in the *women's studies*
department. Which is like, really?

AMBER

And then Leslie is like "but are you sure you clearly expressed
your 'lack of affirmative consent'? This is, after all, a very
serious accusation, young lady" and he's staring at me hard,
like it would suit him just fine if I walked right on out of his
office and his life, and for the first time I flash back to the
night in question and to the way I felt the next morning, how
I wanted to get out of Tom's room as quickly as humanly
possible, and dig a hole and just live there forever, and I'm
like "I'm sure, Leslie, but thank you for reiterating the gravity
of my actions."

TOM

He puts his hand on my shoulder and is like "call me if
you need anything" and I have the sensation I always have
when someone tries to be paternal, which is pretty much
uncontrollable rage mixed with deep-seated resentment and
I brush his hand off my shoulder as though it was a bug and
he flinches like I hit him or something.

AMBER

Linda is also there with me, at the trial. She's my lawyer.
That creeper Leslie told me I could bring one person with
me to any discussion related to the investigation – a friend, a
relative, an advisor or a lawyer. So duh I go with a lawyer.

TOM

I am all alone. I don't even tell my mother about this.
It reminds me of this time in 9th grade when my mom came
to see me in the school play and she got all dressed up and
was so proud but the thing is – I never stepped foot on that
stage. I was in the third floor computer room making out
with this girl Julia, who was also in the chorus and when we
realized we missed the beginning we didn't know what to do
so we just stayed there and later my mom was like "you were
just so good in that play." And I never told her it wasn't true.

AMBER

Bob found Linda for me. He's a lawyer too and needs to feel
important so he's always like "lemme help you with that". Bob
is this tiny man and so maybe he has to compensate. I don't
know what my mom was thinking. It might seem weird to say
so, but my dad was a very attractive man. Even when he was
frail. Like I once overheard my mom on the phone snorting
and saying "well, at least he's still virile." Which is not really
the way you want to think about your dad. Or maybe it is?

TOM

I think I went to a debate in the first week of school in
this room. It was on whether or not Guantanamo Bay was
constitutional, and this one dude was so crazy passionate about
it being unconstitutional that I started to agree with the other
side, just because they weren't so annoying, and the whole
time then and the whole time now I'm like how do you defend
yourself? Is it what you say or how you say it?

AMBER

So when we're all there –

TOM

The chair of the panel stands up and says "Welcome, all."
As though we're at a church service or something.

AMBER and TOM

"Welcome."

TOM

We're here today to decide whether or not Thomas Anthony
committed a violation of the sexual misconduct policy on October
23rd in connection with his interactions with his fellow student –

AMBER and TOM

"Amber Cohen."

AMBER

And when they say my name it's like, whoa. This is really
happening.

TOM

Then I guess we're each supposed to make a statement. I am
made aware of this because the panel chair is like "Tom. Amber.
Now you will each make a statement."

AMBER

Here's a statement for you: the beginning of college was
INSANE. I can barely remember it, that's how insane it was.

I drank. A lot. Like, a lot a lot. And it tastes so foul but you
just keep drinking it.

It's not peer pressure so much as fear. Like, if I don't do this,
I might have to think about who I am and where I am and all
of that is just too...

It was nice to be on the squash team, because you have this
kind of...this built-in group of friends. Or at least people who
could be your friends if you liked them. I mean, you see them
all the time. The thing about doing a sport in college is that
you do it all the time.

And, like, Heather was on the team too and she lived on my hall, so it actually would have been like weird and conspicuous if we *weren't* friends.

And Heather came from a lot of money. You could just tell. And that's not a knock on her at all, it was just…you could tell.

And she had a boyfriend from home, Dave, who was at Georgetown now, and she was always getting WhatsApp messages from him and laughing hysterically. I guess Dave was really funny or something.

I don't know. Heather and I spend a lot of time together, and she shows me how I've been plucking my eyebrows all wrong and she shows me how to drink demurely from a flask. Also she buys me a flask.

We go out every night because everyone goes out every night. And then you go to classes and then you read – and there is so much to read; every day you have like hundreds of pages assigned but you only have between let's say 4 and 7 to do all that reading because after 7 you have to go out and drink 'til you're sick but those afternoon hours are exactly when, if you're on a team, you're at practice. So there's no time to do any of that reading and it starts to build up and even by the end of the first week there's this voluminous amount of reading you haven't done and this equally voluminous terror and *that's* what keeps you drinking.

TOM

Amber makes a really brief statement about how regrettable this whole thing is and how she wishes it hadn't come to this. And I'm like, you know, if you wished that you had it in your power to make it happen.

AMBER

And then Tom makes his statement. He's like a.) we were drunk and b.) I would never rape someone. He can't even say "rape" – he takes this enormous pause before he says it like there's something in his mouth that's causing him great pain but which would be even more painful if it managed to escape.

TOM

I don't want to be here. It's all that goes through my head.
I don't want to be here.

AMBER

I don't like that Tom is all alone. He's like all alone at this long
table.

TOM

I start thinking about when I first got to school, and how...
yeah, how nervous I was. I mean, nobody brought me to
college. My mom didn't, like, come with me and unpack my
clothes and make my bed for me. Nobody took me to the store
to buy that sticky-stuff you use to put up posters, that doesn't
leave a mark on the walls. Nope, I took the bus and then
dragged myself and two crappy suitcases across campus.

And then halfway across the quad, one of those shitty suitcases
just cracks wide open so there I am gathering as much of my
stuff as I can in my arms and trying to look like it doesn't
matter one bit. Finally this guy who's like the Indian Channing
Tatum or something comes over and is like "need a hand?"
and that was Sunil. He went and got me some garbage bags
and we shoved everything into them so I show up to my room
hauling what looks like this gigantic load of trash, but, you
know, it's how I met the best friend I ever had, so I guess, in a
way, I'm grateful.

Not that Sunil and me were tight from the start. I didn't see
him again for a week, and it was possibly the weirdest week
in my life, when you're sort of trying to fit in but you're not
sure yet you even want to. I mean, seriously – part of you just
wants to put all your stuff in your one remaining suitcase and
go back the way you came. It's overwhelming – people are *all
over you* to join their newspaper or their Motown-only a capella
group, or the Black Student Union and you feel sort of sorry
for them and also guilty for not wanting any of it. I mean,
you're just like trying to figure out where the damn bathrooms
are. And how to get from your room to where you can *eat*
things.

21

And yeah, maybe you kinda miss home. Or not like, home, but the idea of it.

Like, maybe you start to realize you've moved on from something. And you're never going back.

AMBER

Linda, my lawyer, told me not to mention enjoying myself for some of the night. So I didn't say anything about my emotional state. About how just looking at Tom makes me tingly all over, so much so that sometimes I need to go home and change my underwear, which is gross but also a totally natural phenomenon as any high school health teacher would have you know. I didn't say that every night, I imagined Tom slipping into my dorm room, unannounced, crawling into my bed and just having me.

TOM

Oh, and thank you Princeton. I almost forgot. They gave me a black roommate. Wasn't that thoughtful? Only Jayson was from San Francisco and into, like, fashion and didn't know a thing about music. He was always telling me how I could "dress for success", which apparently meant never wearing any of the clothes I actually owned, and of course I assumed he was gay so on one of the first nights I'm like "so what's it like being gay?" and he gives me this weird look. Whatever. I'm sure he figured it out sooner or later.

So at the end of that first week the only thing I wanted was to find a piano and be alone. I'm hungover from all the Jell-o shots; I can't get the taste of keg beer outta my mouth; I can't find my jacket which I musta left somewhere. So I'm cold and I have this headache and so far the food – it's like there is just never enough food to fill me up, or I feel like I have to leave the dining hall because I have a sense that I need to do something but almost immediately after I've left I realize I'm starving.

I'm just feeling depleted, you know? And my mom sounds a little tired on the phone, like not as interested in what's going on with me as I would expect. But whatever. If I find a piano, I'll be okay.

So I'm wandering like a jackass up and down Nassau Street
looking for Woolworth, the music department, which isn't
even on that street but me and maps, we do not get along –
when I hear my name. And it's Sunil. And he's leaning against
a wall under this stone arch and he's like "you have to hear
this" and he shoves his iPhone at me and I kid you not the
guy is listening to Mozart's Piano Concerto No. 9, which is
one of my all-time all-time favorites. And he's like "isn't that
astonishing?" And it was.

AMBER

And then they start asking questions. And the questions are
almost as embarrassing as the answers.

TOM

The white dude is like: you're saying it was consensual?
And I'm like, yeah…what I can remember was consensual.
That's right.

AMBER

And then the art professor asks how much I had to drink and
when I drank and how much time elapsed between drinks.
And I wanna be like – that's the point of drinking! So you
don't remember how many drinks you've had and how much
time has elapsed between drinks. But I know I can't say that.

TOM

Some of the questions we wrote ahead of time to ask each other.

AMBER

I think this must be one of Tom's questions: Amber, did you
feel you had something to prove that night? And I'm like "no."
And Linda puts her hand on my knee, which is her way of
saying "no need to elaborate." But when I think about it,
I guess I think that when I got to school I should've said I had
a boyfriend at home because *Heather* got to be this outside
observer, staring down at us all. And by night ten or twelve
the pressure is huge and Heather was always next to me going
"what about him?" and invariably pointing to some loser and
I'd be like "*that's* what you think of me?" but end up hooking
up with him anyway just to get her off my back.

TOM

They ask whether anything else was going on with me that
might have contributed to my behavior that night. And
because Amber isn't really answering the questions, I'm just
like, "nope." Nothing else going on with me.

AMBER

I look at him, and I'm like "really Tom?" Because it really really
seemed like something was going on with him. That night.

TOM

Sunil is like my spirit guide, my maestro, my first base coach,
my brother. I follow him around like a fuckin' cat in heat.
I just have this *reverence* for the guy.

He's from Florida, some town where he was the only person
under, like, ninety-five for miles around, and his family owns
a few restaurants now but for so many years they were just
poor, just like dirt poor. His dad couldn't get work and at one
point his mom and one of his sisters moved back to India.
They went back to *India* because shit was gonna be better
there. So Sunil was left with his dad. They literally started with
a cart. One of those food carts and the two of them cooked
everything and it took years but then it caught on.

He said the violin saved him. He played it all his life. And to
hear him play is a fucking miracle. That's how good he is.

You know how some people love a book and they read it
again and sorta get new things out of it? That never really
happened to me. But with music. With music, it happens all
the time. And Sunil. He wasn't anything like me but he got
that and so he was completely like me.

And it occurred to me how lucky it was that I didn't realize,
growing up, you know, like, how alone I'd been.

I tried to explain it, on the phone, to my mom, and she was
just like "Tommy, you had friends. You've always had friends"
so yeah, she didn't get it.

And you know, she was just sounding so tired.

24

But then I thought it was just that I was so fatigued myself because I wasn't sleeping because, you know, every night it was one of these parties, or three of them. And every night I was having sex.

AMBER

I notice him for the first time in Intro Psych. He's sitting off to my left, a couple rows ahead of me, and his head is jerking forward every few minutes in that way that happens when you can't stay awake. He's making a really valiant effort though and at one point I see him literally hold his eyes open with his fingers and he is also constantly shifting in his chair. So all of that catches my attention, and also, and this probably sounds, like...but yeah, that he's black. I notice that too.

TOM

At some point Sunil is like "man, you should slow it down." And I'm like "why?" And he points out – because *he's* a nice guy – that a couple times, these girls have sent these crazy transparent messages like "hey, did I maybe leave a lip gloss in your room?" or "I wasn't gonna get in touch but I had this weird dream last night and you were in it!" but I'm like screw that. I'm a freshman. It's the first month of school.

And instead I start to get on him about why he's *not* hooking up. Because these girls are just there for the picking and every night he hangs back. I'm like "dude, what're you doing??" and one night he says he's not feeling well and another night he has a leg cramp and another night he doesn't see anyone "remotely interesting". And I'm like "interesting? These girls don't gotta be interesting." And I can tell there's some part of him that thinks I'm a dick and also some part of him that likes that about me. But he doesn't give in. He's just like "Tommy-boy, you do your thing. I'm heading home." And after five nights of that, I pounce. I'm drunk off my ass and I get in his face, like "yo, what the fuck are you doing? This isn't gonna happen every day for the rest of your life, you know" and by this point we've walked out onto the quad and I'm so wasted that I'm seeing stars or maybe there really are that many stars over New Jersey, and I am so pissed at him and love him

like a brother – maybe even more than my actual brothers –
that I am shaking him a little, like shaking his shoulders and
feeling really righteous and like I'm helping a brother out and
teaching him what's right while at the same time justifying all
the choices that *I've* ever made, that when he kisses me I am
more shocked and repulsed and freaked out than I've ever
been in my entire life.

AMBER

But, like, I'm a big fan of black people. I don't want to be so
naïve as to say Jews and African-Americans have all this stuff
in common, but they have some stuff in common, like not
really wanting to go camping, or to Nantucket, and also the
deep and unwavering fear that at any moment they will be
rounded up and killed.

And like, I just, I notice him. That's all.

TOM

The weird thing is that after Sunil like *assaults* me with his tongue,
we're actually okay.

We don't even talk about it.

I mean, it was clear that I didn't want anything to do with any
of that, but he didn't seem hurt or anything. Which is actually
kind of amazing, right? And I start to have a little insight. Like
maybe this is why guys do that. Something doesn't work out,
you just move on. Not like every single female I have ever
known who is physically incapable of moving on even if you
make out once for five minutes on a fucking dance floor.

AMBER

After I notice him in Intro Psych, I start seeing him
everywhere. I turn around and he's a few people behind me
in line in the dining hall with like five waffles on his tray; he's
walking across the quad with this ripped Indian guy, who looks
kinda like Channing Tatum if he was Indian, like he's really
bulked up, which you don't expect with Indian guys no offense.

TOM

And then one day at the end of Intro Psych, Sunil's like "dude, you *are* aware of the fact that this girl can't stop staring at you" and I'm like "who?" and he points to someone a couple rows behind me and she's really hot, like kind of a Chrissy Teigen/ Kate Upton type, skinny but with enormous tits, and I'm like "wow" and he's like "no, the one next to her" and the one next to her is not as good, but you know, I'm equal opportunity.

AMBER

I see him sleeping in Firestone, the library, and I see him in the doorway of PJ's Pancake House, and I see him at the gym where he's maybe technically lifting weights but mostly just talking to that Indian guy. One night I see him making out with this tiny Korean girl at T.I. and he's so into it it's like he's *eating* her face, and normally I would think that was gross but for some reason this time I *don't*.

TOM

So I go and talk to her. Why not, right?

AMBER

He comes up to me after Psych and is just like, "hey."

TOM

And she's like, "hey."

AMBER

And it occurs to me that maybe he's been seeing me everywhere too!

(A new disappointing discovery.)

And maybe he thinks I've been stalking him??
And then I get self-conscious. And *then* I think that maybe actually he's talking to Heather, and I just hugely embarrassed myself, but no…it really does seem like he's talking to me.

TOM

For some reason, I lose my smooth. Like, I don't know what to say next. And we kinda stare at each other until finally I'm like: "So how's psych treating you?"

27

                          AMBER

Oh! It's okay.

                          TOM

Yeah?

                          AMBER

Yeah.

                          TOM

Cool.

                          AMBER

Yeah.

        (Beat.)

                          TOM

So, so far we're having a really interesting conversation.

Sunil's right behind me and kinda jumps in. He makes a bad
joke, at least I think it's a joke?, about how we're probably
missing out on some critical exploration of the human
condition by always falling asleep in this lecture so maybe she
could help fill us in, and I'm thinking, holy shit, Sunil is NOT
good at talking to the ladies. And then this girl, this – sorry –
kinda mousy girl who looks like she could be any of the girls
at Carpenter whose Bat Mitzvahs I went to every weekend
of 8th grade – this girl turns to me and is like "I'm afraid you
might have gotten the impression that I've been following
you or something" – which by the way I hadn't, *at all* – "but
I really have just been struck by how we seem to move along
the same paths or in the same circles or something, like I saw
you in the gym and at PJ's and weren't you at the Bent Spoon
too – the ice cream place? And isn't it crazy" and all that and
I'm just, like, who is this girl??

Then her friend, the hot one, is like "Amber, I think he just
wants your notes" and poor Amber turns beet fucking red
and you can see her mind just unraveling. She's like:

"Oh, right, duh."

TOM

And then these kinda splotchy spots start to appear all over
her neck and before I can even help it I'm like "nah, I wasn't
after yer notes. I saw you that time, at the Bent Spoon, right?"
even though I haven't once gotten ice cream since I got here
and would never pay five dollars for a tiny scoop of gourmet
anything, but I don't know what's up with me; I keep going:
"and I was thinking we could go back there together, like on
purpose this time."

AMBER

The funny thing or maybe it was just weird was that I'd never
actually seen him at the ice cream place. As soon as I said it
I knew it was wrong; I was just running at the mouth the way
I do sometimes, and sometimes as a result not everything
I say is one hundred percent wholly and completely true.
I mean, maybe it's just that ice cream is never far from my
mind. Or maybe I just wanted it to be true but either way we
do end up getting ice cream the next day and he offers to buy
mine, which even though I demur because I'm the product of
feminists who worked really hard to have the right to buy their
own ice cream, the offer means we're on a real date, right? Me
and 'Thomas Anthony', who, I mean, even his name is hot,
and who knows, maybe he's gonna be my first real boyfriend,
not counting my camp boyfriend, which in all honesty was
a relationship based almost entirely on correspondence.
Anyway I can't really believe it, and I'm trying not to think
about all the other things I should be doing, like seriously the
call of those books stacked on my desk is deafening, and also
I didn't work out as hard as I usually do this afternoon, I don't
know why, and now this ice cream that I can't help but eat all
of is gonna make me fat, I can feel myself getting fatter as I eat
it, not that I have eating issues, I mean, I don't, aside from the
way all girls have eating issues, which is that we think about
what we eat 100% of the time and always wanna kill ourselves.

TOM

Okay, so she's, like, weird.

I mean, she talks fast, like Usain Bolt-fast, and she doesn't really look at me.

But she's not shy, exactly. I've been with shy girls before. This isn't really shy. This is more like...yeah, weird, I guess.

AMBER

But it doesn't matter. I'm on a date with this guy who for some reason I noticed and it turned out he noticed me too, and *this* is why I'm here, right? For experience, not just to read, like, books I'll forget a month after reading them, and life is short, I know it is; I've had that feeling in my gut since I was a little kid, and it's not just because my dad was older and was always maybe about to die, it's something that was in me, was just *in* me, this sense that you can't hold onto anything and every moment is over before it's even begun.

TOM

Not like there's something wrong with her. She's just *awkward* and I'd like to say I find it cute or something, but really I just feel awkward too, until she's like "god, I'm so awkward, aren't I" and without meaning to I'm like "yeah, I guess" and she apologizes and laughs in this way that *is* kinda cute and says she's gonna stop eating her ice cream because she's SO full, and she puts it down, but a minute or two later she picks it up and finishes it anyway.
And then she's like:

AMBER

So what's up with your friend?

TOM

What?

AMBER

That hot Indian guy.

TOM

You mean Sunil?

AMBER

How many hot Indian guys do you hang around with?

TOM

And for a second I'm sorta taken aback, like despite myself,
because does she think Sunil is hotter than me?
But then she adds:

AMBER and TOM

Not that he's hotter than you, Thomas Anthony.

TOM

I mean, she is already calling me *Thomas Anthony*! Which
is something only my mom has called me, and only when
she's mad or like being really lovey with me, but this weird
girl starts it up right away, which is what I mean when I said
she wasn't really shy; I mean, she's actually kinda straight up
confident except that she can't look me in the eye and she
can't stop talking.

AMBER

A little thing about Judaism? When something good happens
to you, you just assume something bad is on the way. That's
the way Jews exist in the world, and also we have a very
hard time walking around knowing about all the bad things
happening at every moment in every part of the world, like
if you watch that Naomi Watts movie about the tidal wave in
2004, then afterwards you're gonna Google the *shit* out of it
and find this real account of a guy who stayed up in a *tree* for
hours while he watched everyone he knew get swept away, at
which point you can't stop thinking about the last moments
those people had alive and their fear, and also the pain they
left in their wake. When this kid I didn't know well, but had
known since preschool, so I *knew* him, you know?…when
he killed himself in 11th grade, it occurred to me just how
deafening and enormous the grief must be that emanates off
the surface of this earth. Like, our atmosphere must just be
filled with all this airless sorrow.

TOM

"Is he a nerd in a not nerd's body?" She's *still* talking about
Sunil, and I really don't wanna be thinking about his body
right now, I mean cool it, girl, who just took you for ice
cream?, so I'm like "nah, he's chill" and she's like "okay but,
like, didn't I notice he had a violin case" and so then I have
to get into the whole music thing and she's all "wow. WOW,
you two sound like professional musicians. So is that why you
came to Princeton? To pursue music?" And she's looking at
me in this way that I can't explain and before I know it I'm
saying "I can't think about music like it's work because I need
something in my life that's an escape from everything else."
I mean, I tell this girl that I need to *escape*. And she nods like
she understands, and then says: "so why did you come here?"
Which to me is, like, obvious: because I aced my SATs, and
I got in; you don't *not* go to Princeton, and she's like "I was
attracted to the university's very strong English and creative
writing department. See, my only minor talent is in writing
so I have to pursue that path because really I think we pursue
what we feel we're decent at because why set ourselves up for
total abject failure." That's what Amber Cohen is like.

AMBER and TOM

I'm telling you.

AMBER

Like after that kid died, and his name was Jonathan, I feel like
I should say his name, I was Skyping with Rachel about how
horrible it was, how we just felt empty and like we had no
business being alive, when one of my camp friends messaged
me too, wondering if I could send her a photo of me from the
summer after 9th grade because she was about to get that same
haircut and wanted to show her stylist, so I'm having these
two simultaneous conversations, one about the utter existential
pain of living and the other about whether that was my haircut
after 9th grade or maybe she means the one during the 10th
grade chorus trip to Budapest? and really that just about sums
up life, doesn't it?

Only it doesn't. Because it leaves out so much. Like when my
dad died, I was just numb for so long. For so long I walked
through my life without really living it, just years of school,
squash, homework, in this endless cycle, and feeling like if I
had something great to say there wouldn't be anyone there
to hear it because my dad was many things – a product of his
time and of growing up Jewish in a tiny town in the South,
which probably made him irascible and insecure but he would
always listen to me and seemed to care what I had to say and
when he was gone that was gone too. And somewhere deep
inside, I think I felt like I was due for something good to
happen, and when I got into Princeton it seemed like maybe
that was my dad's doing, like a balancing of the scales.

TOM

Never in the past, not once, yo, have I gotten such a hard time
for *not* making a move on a date. I mean, I went with her for
fucking ice cream, for godsake.

AMBER

But Thomas Anthony felt like too much. I mean not only was he
by far the hottest person who had ever noticed me, but behind
that layer of swagger and charm, he was also frankly the nicest.

All of which is to say, he didn't kiss me that night. And I couldn't
tell what that meant. I mean, maybe it was because all we'd done
was get ice cream like fifth graders so afterwards it made sense to
go our separate ways.

Or…maybe it was…me.
Something to do with me.

TOM

An *hour* later, I get this message on Facebook:

"Dear Tom."

AMBER
(With a bashful smile.)

I couldn't help myself.

33

TOM

"Just to be clear, I really enjoyed hanging out with you.
I wasn't sure, based on the way our date (Was it even a date?)
ended – the way you said "okay, so see ya around" that you
would wanna see me again but I wanted to let you know that
I'd be more than game to give it another go because I feel like
I still have so much to teach you about the world, Thomas
Anthony, like the proper way to eat an ice cream cone (Which
is not all in one bite.) and how to pronounce your linguistics
teacher's name. (I spent a summer in Wales.) And if that
doesn't tempt you completely, I don't know what will.

AMBER

I was really torn about the use of an emoticon, which any self-
respecting person should be, but then again I was torn about
sending the message at all, so I figured what the hell.
Also the hour I spent writing that message was more time than
I'd spent focused on any single thing up to that point in my
college career.

TOM

I don't know if I'd been planning to go out with her again.
Probably not, if I'm being honest. Some guys get off on a girl
being aggressive but for me it's the other way around. If I'm
being honest. Like, you know, let ME make the moves.

But in the case of Amber, I remembered this thing she'd said
when we were ordering our ice cream, like "isn't it funny
how incapacitating having choices is" or something like that,
and also she isn't quite as, like, mousy as I first thought, like
actually her eyes are sorta weird and sad and pretty when she
actually looks at you, and the one time she actually looked at
me, when I was saying goodbye, I was so taken aback that I
just took off.

So I wrote her back. I mean, I waited a week, but I wrote her back.

AMBER

He waited *a week*. And, like, I saw him around and had to
pretend I hadn't written that stupid thing.

TOM

Sunil was like, "dude, you're blowing her off" and he seemed
really amused by the whole thing, and strangely, like,
interested in Amber. Like in what I knew about her, and
I was like "I don't know, dude, she's just sort of a weirdo"
and he's like "but you like her" and I'm like "I don't know."
And he seems really suspicious about why I haven't had a real
relationship before and I'm like dude I'm eighteen; I don't
need to settle down. And he's like "but I bet your mom would
like if you did" and I don't know how he knows that, but my
mom *is* always like "Thomas, you could make some young
lady so happy, why do you insist on torturing these women?"
But I can't admit that so I'm just like, "get off my back" and
then he says, really simply, "what are you looking for, man?
What do you think you're gonna find?" And I almost tell
him the truth, which is that I have this sort of 3am fear, this
desperate like night of the soul fear, that I will never really
find my way around this world and that whatever I do I won't
amount to anything…

And this might be why I write Amber back. Because she
looked at me as though I really might pursue something.

AMBER

He Snapchats me: "Amber, wanna meet at Cap tonight? Kegger."
And I can't help it. I write back

AMBER and TOM

right away

TOM

I get a message back. Like, within two minutes.
This girl has no fucking game, right?
But that's okay, I guess. I mean, so she has no game. So what.

AMBER

I don't know what to wear so I just go with a sort of tried
and true look – the tank under a blazer with tight jeans and
tall boots look. And I used the more expensive of my two
shampoos and I even read two pages of my psych textbook
before going out and they happened to be about the pratfall

effect which explains why people actually are *attracted* to people who aren't perfect, who are clumsy or flawed in some way, and I found that really encouraging and the timing, like, really fateful.

And that afternoon I'd spoken to my mom, which is hit or miss because sometimes she only talks about herself, which is my fault for asking her so many questions but I always want to see if she'll realize she hasn't asked me anything and turn it towards me of her own accord. But this time I think there was some undeniable quality in me – happiness, I guess – and she could just tell and she was like "Amber?" and I said, "you know, I think I'm gonna like it here" which is obviously a quote from *Annie*, a movie I watched about a zillion times when I was a kid, so much so that I think the movie and my childhood are sort of synonymous. Which made her cry a little. To think of me happy. Because that's just not always true. Of me.

TOM

Right before I'm supposed to meet up with Amber, I'm pre-gaming with Sunil. We're three shots of Jagermeister and a couple Sam Adams in when my phone rings and it's my mom – and she's just like "Tommy, I've got it." The big fucking C. Cancer. She says she doesn't want me to give it a single thought and she's fine; it's not such a bad kind of cancer and I should enjoy college and I'm like you know I can't do that and she starts to cry and she says "Tommy, what'll kill me quicker than cancer is if you don't take every advantage of your time at school" and what can I say to that? My brothers didn't go to college, my dad – nope – and the closest my mom came was three months of nursing school. So she's wailing and I'm all "okay, okay, of course I'll enjoy college" so I'm trying and Sunil and I go back to pre-gaming and talking and I'm already kinda drunk and it comes out, what she just told me, and Sunil – he just flat out bursts into tears. I mean, *I'm* not even crying but he cries for me and for my mom, who he's never even met and that moves me – that fuckin' moves me – and our man Mozart is playing in the background, Piano Concerto

number 9, and Sunil puts his arms around me and I start to
let it out; I let it out because I can't lose my mom; I can't lose
my mom; she's been the glue binding me to this earth, I know
it even if I've never said it out loud…and it's good to be held,
it's nice to be held by my friend, to be in his arms; I even have
this passing thought about how nice it must be to be Sunil's
violin, this is how gentle he is, and even when he, like, rubs
my back, that's okay; he's just there for me; he's just feeling it,
but yeah…

When he tries to kiss me again… I mean, that's too much,
that's a line crossed, that's me being taken advantage of right
there and so I say so; I jump back and I say so, and he's like
"Tommy. Come on, Tommy. You know you're in love with
me. It's okay. We're in love."

AMBER

Heather walked me to Cap even though I told her not to,
and when we get there I'm waiting for her to leave. I just don't
want to be with her when Tom arrives. Like I don't need a.)
the comparison and b.) the suggestion that I didn't want to
meet him on my own. I didn't want to seem nervous. Precisely
because I was so nervous.

But Heather isn't getting the picture. So finally I have to just
be like, "so maybe you should go now?" at which point she
gets really huffy and is like "suit yourself" and as she walks off
adds "nothing's gonna happen tonight anyway" which, like,
infuriates me, because how does she know that? And so I call
after her "who died and made you Humbert Humbert?" and
then to clarify, "an omniscient narrator" and she looks back at
me like "what??" and walks away.

TOM

And then there's this long pause and finally I'm like nope.
Nope you've got that wrong. I say you don't know the first
thing about me and you never will. I say you're an asshole
and a fag and my mom has cancer and what the fuck were
you thinking? And I can't help it but I pick up his violin
and I smash it; I smash it into the ground and pieces of it fly

everywhere and Sunil screams as though I've hit him, or worse, and my mother is sick and my friend, my only friend, is not my friend anymore and I wanna puke it all up and get it out of my body, just out, just gone, all of it, and then cleaned up and away, I want someone else to please clean it up – please.

AMBER

I was standing in the quad, waiting, taking little ladylike sips from my flask and watching this kid – like he was definitely too young to be a freshman – walk along the fence but he kept falling off it so it wasn't really so impressive but still strangely compelling – to watch someone keep failing at something – and I was like nota bene, Amber. The pratfall effect at work again. How human it is to fail.

TOM

I don't know why but I kept thinking about Richard Wright's *Black Boy*. We read it in 10th grade English. Like you know, even the title. Even the title alone. I felt like everyone was looking at me because, you know, they were. I mean, there were other kids from "under-served communities" who got into Carpenter through this program Prep but my year I was the only guy. And so most of my friends were white. And no. I never told them that I felt at all…like, weird, going to their houses after school and playing Xbox while their black babysitters cooked and cleaned and made us dinner.

And in English class we'd read aloud. And I remember having to read this part of *Black Boy* that was like: "I live in this country where black people's aspirations are limited. So I had to go somewhere else to do something to redeem my being alive." *To redeem my being alive.* I remember that part. And I felt so much shame. And I felt so much shame that I felt so much shame.

AMBER

When Tom got there I could immediately tell he was in a bad way. And in my head I was like "please don't end this. Don't say you have to go home. Please." I tried to just keep him drinking so he wouldn't leave. And, amazingly, that worked and eventually we went inside and danced. He had his hand on my waist and he was kind of holding on. Digging

in. As though if he let go something horrible would happen.
And I liked it. Feeling needed like that. But I think I also knew
that something wasn't right? And it made me so sad, that Tom
might be sad. I mean what in the world should make Tom sad?

TOM

And suddenly she just takes her shirt off.

AMBER

I mean, yeah I was drunk, but I'd been drunk before and
never done that. I just had to do something to get rid of that
look in his eyes.

TOM

I was like *what is going on.* Did we just walk into some alternate
fucking universe where Amber Cohen takes her top off?... But
she looked happy. And free... To this day, I'm not sure I've
ever felt free like that.

AMBER

We were in this crush of people. We were inside of it and
moving with it and I loved it because I don't usually feel...part
of things in that way. And being there with Tom. That was like.

TOM

She looked...yeah, she looked sexy, and I was like, let's get
out of here.

AMBER

And I took his hand and led him away. I felt like a character in
someone else's story: Daisy and Gatsby, or that woman who
worked at the department store in season one of *Mad Men* and
Don Draper. I was just a girl pulling an attractive man out of a
party with her.

TOM

Where do you wanna go?

AMBER

Where do *you* wanna go?

TOM

I think I must've said we could go back to my place.

AMBER

But first we just walked around. And made out. All over
campus. It was…amazing. I remember my hand in his, and
the total thrill of wondering when we'd kiss next combined
with the equal thrill of knowing it was going to happen.
The *gift* of that.

TOM

When we got to my room, Jayson was there, sleeping; I must've
thought he was sleeping. Or maybe I just wasn't thinking about
Jayson.

AMBER

He was sleeping. And we sort of tiptoe in, trying not to laugh.
But there's this enormous poster on the wall, this Calvin Klein
ad with Justin Bieber like naked, and I'm like what? And Tom
is like "that is NOT mine I swear" and that cracks me up, and
his roommate was like "shut the fuck up I'm trying to sleep"
and then Tom was kissing me again.

TOM

I remember these little flashes of what came next… Her back,
this streak of white. And the light going on in the room, but I
don't know who turned it on. I remember how good it felt to
turn off my mind. The way you feel when you get lost inside
a piece of music and the texture of it just envelops you and
you're not in the world anymore; you're just part of the music.

AMBER

I remember the weight of him on top of me and thinking
he was different from Zach – not necessarily heavier, just
different, like he was giving me more of himself, letting his
weight just completely cover me up. I remember kissing him.
I remember at some point really kissing him and thinking
this guy was an excellent excellent kisser and worrying
a little about that tuna sandwich I'd had at lunch while
feeling simultaneously proud of myself for experiencing this
unexpected thing, and very lucky.

Yeah. I think mostly I just felt really lucky.

TOM

The Latino one only uses the word coitus, not sex. Did Amber
say anything, she asks, trying to sound neutral, when you were
mid-coitus? Not that I remember, I tell them, always trying
to smile as though I'm Mister fuckin' Rogers over here.
How about "actually" the women's studies woman suggests.
Did she say "actually" at any point?

AMBER

There was this moment when suddenly it all just felt a little
bit...wrong.

TOM

No, I don't remember what she said or if she said anything
but yeah, she probably didn't say yes. But, like, who says yes?
Who in these situations is like "yes do that, please." We were
drunk. She was into it...

And if she wasn't into it at some point...well then my body, my
brain, convinced me she was. I wasn't knowingly... I didn't do
anything knowingly... I know that.

AMBER

Why would you have asked him to stop? You were into it at
first. On this everyone agrees. And I really think about this.
This zone of wanting something and not wanting it at the
same time. Like I didn't ask Zach Lieberman to stop, and
it's not like he was so gentlemanly. And now I am always
silent during sex. I didn't ask Robby O'Neill in the 8th grade
not to put his fingers inside of me on a dare in a closet, even
though his thumbnail dug into me and it killed. I didn't say
stop in 5th grade when Rachel and these two other girls were
pulling my hair to see how long I could take it. I didn't say
stop when my high school advisor suggested I take French
and Latin and Ancient Greek *and* Japanese my junior year,
even though when it comes down to it I much prefer English
to any foreign language because how can you express yourself
fully in a language that isn't your own? It's hard enough to
express yourself in your own language. I didn't say stop when
my mother told me not to eat carbohydrates if I ever wanted

to get married. I didn't say stop when my dad died because
I knew that was one thing I couldn't stop even if I tried, but
still... I didn't even

AMBER and TOM

Try

TOM

to remember what happened next they keep asking. And I
am trying. But I can't get this moment out of my brain, this
moment in the really early morning, when I woke up, and
my face was tangled in her hair, like it was in my mouth and
stuff. She was sleeping. Peacefully. And I saw the condom
wrapper on the floor and was breathing a sigh of relief because
I thought shit, Tom, you were so gone, something bad coulda
happened. And then she opens her eyes and when she sees me
she kinda startles a little, like she'd forgotten where she was.
Then it's like she's about to say something but instead she just
throws up all over the floor, just everywhere.

AMBER and TOM

"I'm so sorry"

TOM

She keeps saying:

AMBER and TOM

"I'm so sorry"

TOM

And I'm holding her hair back and I see just a little of the back
of her neck and I swear I wanna, like, touch it, just a tiny bit
with my thumb, which is weird because there she is puking
but I feel something, like a longing for... Like maybe I do
actually like this girl. After that she runs outta there pretty
quick but I'm thinking she's embarrassed. And I clean it all up.
It's fucking disgusting but I don't mind too much.

At some point, Jayson walks in like he's been up for hours
already and run ten miles and designed a new messenger bag
or some shit, and he's like, "good night?" in this snide little
Jayson way and I don't say anything, and he's like "next time

try not to fuck someone when I'm literally in the top bunk," and I'm like "I'm sorry, man," which I really was, and then, just to be sure, I say, "but she was into it, right?" And he gives me this look like "you're really gonna ask me that?" but still he said "well, she wasn't *not* into it, if that's what you're asking." And I *guess* that was what I was asking. And I was relieved.

AMBER

At one point during the trial they start reading our text messages.

TOM

Like, *out loud.* And let me tell you it is really fucking weird to hear your own idiotic texts read out loud as, like...evidence.

AMBER

Hey Amber. I guess that was kind of weird. Ha. But I hope you're feeling better and you never vomit like that again in your life because that looked like deeply deeply unpleasant.

I'm sorry I was in a sort of weird "frame of mind" yesterday. I hope I didn't freak you out or anything. I'm not really such an asshole. I promise. See you soon. – T.

And the even crazier thing is? I wrote back.

TOM

Hey Tom. No worries. I mean yes it was a little weird but it's okay. I don't think you're an asshole. – A.

So, like.

AMBER and TOM

I don't know.

TOM

But I think: that's gotta score me some points. Her text back to me.

AMBER

And then this awful professor – I've repressed her face she was that awful – I think she was in women's studies so she thinks she and I are...she thinks we are on, like, intimate terms. And she just asks the most graphic questions in the most matter-of-fact way, like "Amber, at what point did you feel Thomas Anthony's penis inside of you?"

43

TOM

Thomas Anthony is what my mom calls me.

AMBER

And "can you go into detail about the moment he ejaculated?"

TOM

Thank god she isn't here. It was bad enough that time we watched *Game of Thrones* together.

AMBER

I mean, let's just be clear. We had sex. And I didn't say, like, "yes, fuck me. Do it in any way you want." So when they ask: "did this boy do this to you without your consent?" even though I might not have chosen that exact phrasing it seemed like the honest answer was yes, especially because I was probably too drunk to give any meaningful consent anyway –

TOM

You think *I* wasn't drunk?

AMBER

And because Olivia, my RA, sat me down after Heather told her and I guess Olivia had been raped once too and she said "Amber you have to take this very seriously. If women don't take this very seriously it hurts all women. It affects all women."

TOM

Jayson comes into the hearing wearing this bow-tie like he's about to go have tea with the queen but what comes out of his mouth is low-down and dirty; he says Amber couldn't have been conscious when we were… He says he didn't hear a thing from her. But I'm like…who would have a better sense of that? Me, or the guy on the top bunk? I think there are things the body just *knows*, you know??

AMBER

And then the assistant dean of students is like, "Amber, I want you to pay very close attention to what I'm about to say" and he looks around the room really intensely like a poor man's Gregory Peck giving his closing statement in *To Kill a Mockingbird* and he says: "So everyone agrees that earlier that

44

night you took your shirt off. That you drank to excess. That
you very willingly went back to Tom's room and got into
his bed. Which makes me wonder: why do you think these
actions that you admit you freely took don't amount to some
kind of tacit consent?" And the panel stares at me, one of the
women looking kind of annoyed with the tenor of the question
as though it doesn't accurately reflect *her* opinion, and the
other one doing her best to appear really neutral–which is
when it occurs to me that maybe it doesn't even matter what
I say. Maybe these people will hear what they want to hear no
matter what. Maybe they decided in the first five minutes what
they thought happened, or even last week. And I'm processing
that and to stall a little I'm just like "what?" And he says "you
heard me" kind of harshly, like a dare. And for the first time
I really wanna leave the room, but I can't, here I am, so I look
down at my hands, and... I tell the truth. Which is that I do
remember it. This moment when all of a sudden he was inside
me, and it's not like I expected him to ask my permission but I
didn't expect him not to either. And it hurt and it kept hurting,
and eventually I just jumped out of bed.

TOM

Wait a second. No you didn't.

AMBER

What?

TOM

You didn't jump out of bed.

AMBER
(Slowly.)

I thought you didn't remember.

TOM

I would remember that.

AMBER

But you don't. You obviously don't because it happened.
I jumped out of bed and you grabbed me, hard, and I was like
"actually, um" but you pulled me back into bed and you just...

TOM

I didn't!

That's a lie – she didn't get out of bed; I know she didn't, and she certainly didn't *jump* out of... Amber, tell them.

AMBER

No I did. I had this strong physical impulse to get away from you, I did –

TOM

What are you talking about?

AMBER

I'm just saying what happened –

TOM

(Not able to help himself.)

You are such a privileged bitch, do you know that?

AMBER

I'm privileged? I am? I bet you've always had friends. You've always had girls in love with you. You've always felt good about how you look. You get to be comfortable in your own body. And that's a privilege. *That's* a privilege.

TOM

It's a privilege to have everyone always looking at you? Is that right, Amber?

AMBER

(Really sincere.)

No one ever looks at me. So yeah. I think it is.

TOM

You're crazy if you think I'm comfortable in my own body.

AMBER

Well if you're not that might explain why you did this to me.

TOM

Why are *you* doing this to me? Because you think I've had it easy or something?

AMBER

I don't think you've had it easy. I think you raped me.

(Long beat.)

TOM

And I hate her. In that moment I really fucking hate her.
And I say so.

AMBER
(Suddenly quiet.)
You don't mean that…do you?

TOM

You're like this…flood of feelings that you just dump at
people's feet. You don't get what it's like to have to be careful;
you don't get that it matters how people see you.

AMBER

I never stop thinking about how other people see me.

TOM

I know I have to calm down but I can't. And I can't hide. Holy
fuck, there is just nowhere to hide! I can't have any body but
this one; I can't be anybody but who I am – this man in the
world who everyone assumes will make a mistake, if they just
wait long enough!

And then Diaz is like "both of you sit down! And, Amber,
speak ONLY to us and explain what happened next. When
you were back in the bed." And Amber, out of breath from
fucking me over, is looking at her hands like they're the most
fascinating things she's ever seen.

AMBER

I don't know how to say out loud what happened next. Which
is that I let him do what he wanted. I mean, I lay there as he
pounded into me, this vacant look in his eyes, just thinking, "you
idiot, Amber" because I'd let myself believe that he actually
liked me. And also "fuck you, Tom" because stupidly I thought
he could see that I'd spent my entire existence feeling…
invisible, and that he would therefore know how amazing it
would be just to look at me right now.

And I felt so profoundly, like desperately...sad, like am I the only one aware of the fact that I'm on this earth, in which case am I really on it? And if I don't exist then who *is* this, what is the point of this brain constantly torturing me with all this self-doubt if there is no self; what is this body I'm inside of, this body I *hate*, that never does what I want it to and doesn't look good in the clothes I put it in, that I don't like to look at too long in the mirror, that seems so wholly inadequate to the task of housing a person in this awful, fucked up world.

And Tom didn't see any of that... He didn't see or forgive anything of my body or my soul. And I wanted to die.

TOM
(With reluctance.)

Yeah, so.
There are things the body just knows.

AMBER
(Then, quietly, realizing.)
So of course I didn't say anything else that night. I wasn't even there.

TOM
(Quietly, a fear/a discovery.)
So maybe I knew. Maybe I knew. That she wasn't...
And that's the... That's the thing that I... I mean, I thought...
Deep down, I thought I was a nice guy.

AMBER
But I'm here, now. And I can't just be silent anymore. I can't do that to myself.

TOM
She's crying, all of a sudden, these sort of animal cries that make everyone deeply uncomfortable.

AMBER
But the cost of not doing that to myself anymore is... Tom.
Which is just...

TOM

I don't like seeing her cry like that. It's all just... It's too much.

AMBER

And then *he* starts to cry, and we just...

AMBER and TOM

So now we're both

TOM

sitting there just...

AMBER

and Tom is all alone and I wanna...

TOM

I mean there's Amber, and she's gazing at me with this
unmistakable...love. Which is like...

AMBER

I remember this Kierkegaard quote we learned in Intro Phil.
"It belongs to the imperfection of everything human that man
can only attain his desire by passing through its opposite."
But I don't know what it means.

(Beat.)

TOM

Isn't it crazy, the idea that every single thing leads to
everything else?

I played the piano for the first time when I was eleven.
This was back at 261, when I was in a class with thirty other
kids, and none of us paid any attention, just no one did
anything anyone told us to, but still this one teacher, Mrs.
Landrieu, still she, like, found me.

Mrs. Landrieu was sweet and in over her head, like all those
kinda offensive movies you see of well-meaning white ladies in
inner city schools trying to control this, like, pack of beasts.

But yeah, we probably were a little like beasts. And she *was*
sweet. And she was trying. And one day towards the end of

49

a particularly, I mean, a particularly fucked up class – Elijah, who was the worst of the worst and also my best friend – might've implied that he was gonna go to her house and mess her up when he was like, "Mrs. Landrieu, I'm gonna go to your house and mess you up."

And then Mrs. Landrieu, she says in this tiny voice: Elijah, go to the office. Go straight to the principal's office, but here's the thing – he won't go. He just stays there. And the whole class laughs. And this is when she starts to cry.

And the next day, Elijah sits right up front, like an asshole, just to show her who's boss. And yeah, it was funny, but the look on her face like she wanted to die right there on the spot made it not the least bit funny. And so when she calls on me – and I'm telling you her voice has gotten even tinier since yesterday – I'm just like "I think that's a really interesting question, Mrs. Landrieu," which doesn't win me any popularity points but, you know, I see a chance to do something nice for someone and I take it.

That's the kind of guy I thought I was, after all.

Of course she wants to talk to me after class. And I think she's gonna thank me but instead she's like: "Tommy, I wondered if you might like piano lessons."

I'm like "what??" Turns out she teaches piano on the side. So when I show up at her apartment the next day and sit next to her on the piano bench – by the way, I had no interest in the *piano*, zero, but I would also never turn down something that's free – that's like my modus fucking operandi – when I sit next to her and she says really gently and really kindly, "I know your father left a few months ago" I just… I break down.

I mean, I didn't even like the guy. I didn't even like the guy.

And…after that, like…what else can you do. So you just play.

> *(Suddenly they are in a scene – the college party that took place the night of the incident. TOM is agitated and irritable. They have to shout a bit to be heard over the music in the quad.)*

                    AMBER
             (Waving awkwardly at him.)
Tom!

                    TOM
Sorry – I got a little held up.

                    AMBER
That's totally fine. I've only been here…
        (Looks at her watch – she's been here forever already.)
Like, yeah, not very long.

    (She holds herself, shivering.)

                    TOM
                (Annoyed.)
You're cold?

                    AMBER
I'm always cold.

    (He rolls his eyes.)

                    TOM
You want a drink?

                    AMBER
Like from, the, um, keg?

                    TOM
Yeah.

                    AMBER
Well, it's so delicious, I don't know how anyone could turn it
down.

                    TOM
                (Peeved.)
Is that a joke or something?

                    AMBER
Are you okay?

TOM

(Angrily.)

Yeah I'm just trying to figure out if you want a beer. Is that okay
by you?

AMBER

You don't seem like you're in the best frame of mind tonight.

TOM

Who talks that way: "the best frame of mind"?

AMBER

I do.

TOM

I know. It's weird.

AMBER

Is it?

TOM

We could also just get outta here.

AMBER

Sure.

I mean, we could go inside and like, dance. Or find another
party. Or get someone to go to Varsity and pick stuff up for us.

TOM

Why would we do that when there are free drinks right here.

AMBER

Good point. We wouldn't. I'm just happy to do what you want
to do.

TOM

I'm gonna get a beer for the road.

AMBER

I also have a, um.

(She pulls out her flask.)

Heather got it for me.

TOM

Heather's the hot one, right?

AMBER

I mean, yes, she is very attractive. Like, objectively attractive.
She has a lot of qualities men would find attractive, I guess.
Like she has a very nice body –

TOM

Can I just... Lemme just see that flask.

(He drinks from it; she drinks from it; this relaxes him.)

That's good. What is that?

AMBER

I'm not sure because Heather just gave it to me so...

TOM

It's tequila.

AMBER

If you knew, why'd you ask?

TOM
(Smiling.)

Maybe I was testing you.

AMBER

Why would you be doing that?

TOM

See if you're up to my super high standards.

AMBER

From what I hear you have no standards at all.

TOM

Now who told you that.

AMBER

I think there's a whole website at Princeton devoted to it.

TOM
(Dry.)

That's hilarious.

AMBER

I thought so.

TOM

What can I say? I like women. That's not a crime.

AMBER

No it's not.

TOM

And I like you.

AMBER
(Out of awkwardness at being complimented.)
So, how much do you know about the pratfall effect?

TOM

What?

AMBER

I was reading about it tonight in our psych book and
it's actually really interesting: it's about how a person's
attractiveness increases or decreases after he or she makes a
mistake. So a highly-competent person, like, say, a celebrity,
would be *more* likable after committing a blunder, while the
opposite would be true if –

TOM

God, do you ever stop talking?

AMBER

What?

TOM
(With a small smile.)

Just stop talking.

AMBER

Okay.

TOM

I'm gonna kiss you now.

AMBER

Oh.
Okay.

> *(He does; it's actually kinda tender. When it's over, AMBER doesn't know what to say.)*

AMBER

Let's play a game. Let's play Two Truths and a Lie.

TOM

Um. No.

AMBER

Come on.

TOM

Okay. I have two truths for you... I hate games and I hate that game.

AMBER

But you'll play it.

TOM

And why would I do that?

AMBER

If you wanna sleep with me tonight, for one thing.

TOM

...who goes first?

> *(A light gray feather falls from above, right in between AMBER and TOM. Before it hits the ground – blackout.)*

End of play.

CPSIA information can be obtained
at www.ICGtesting.com
Printed in the USA
LVHW082049140922
728379LV00002B/356

9 781786 823083